MW01063114

FIRST-TIME HOMEOWNER'S SURVIVAL GUIDE

What You'll Need, What To Know & How To Navigate the World of Homeownership!

By Joshua Harper

Bridge Press

support@bridgepress.org

Please consider writing a review!

Just visit: purplelink.org/review

Copyright 2021. Joshua Harper. All Rights Reserved.

No part of this book may be reproduced or transmitted
in any form or by any means, electronic or mechanical,
including photocopying, recording or by any other form
without written permission from the publisher.

ISBN: 978-1-955149-28-0

TABLE OF CONTENTS

INTRODUCTION

Congratulations, you just bought your first home! How do you feel? Excited? Hopeful? Adult-like? Possibly, but if you're like most first-time homebuyers, what you're really feeling is **fear** — pure, unbridled, feel-it-in-your bones terror.

It's not that you're not excited about owning your own little slice of the world, especially since buying a home is generally considered a sounder financial investment than renting. But, renting comes with its own set of advantages, such as the fact that if anything happens to go wrong with the house, it can be fixed by a single phone call. Now, if something breaks and you have to make *that* phone call, it's going to cost you a little bit of money out of your pocket, and that's a scary thought.

That's why we came up with this book—a "first-time homebuyers survival guide." It is intended to cover some of the most essential things you need to know about your new house, especially if it is your first time owning one. As a disclaimer, we have to mention that there's absolutely no way everything that could possibly happen to your house will be covered inside this book. But, we've tried to include some of the most common things you'll need to know to make sure your house stays in tip-top shape. Fair warning, though, if a herd of angry buffalo stampede through your living room, you're on your own.

In this book, we're going to assume that you've already bought a house, so if you're looking for a guide on navigating a successful mortgage process or how to identify which houses are the best investments, this guide isn't for you. To put this together, we envisioned somebody standing inside of their first house for the first time, looking around, and wondering to themselves, "What do I do now?" If that's you, then keep reading.

Before we get to the nitty-gritty, I want you to take a deep breath. Deeper. Now, let it out. I want you to reflect on the fact that you're entering into a journey that many people refuse to take. Buying a home is a serious financial commitment. For most people, it's the most expensive thing they'll ever buy. Although the average percentage of Americans who actually own a home is going up (currently sitting at 66%), there are still many people who will never even consider buying a home for various reasons, let alone actually buy one.

So, take a few seconds to pat yourself on the back for taking a huge step in your life. It doesn't matter if your first home is 200 square feet or 20,000; it's yours, and that's all that matters.

If you're fortunate enough to have a good support network around you after buying your first home, then you most likely have been prepared in some way for this step. Perhaps you were even thrown a party where your friends and family gave you various tools and items you need to keep your home looking sharp.

If so, those gifts can be a huge help as you begin this part of your life. If not, that's fine too because some of those things you were given you might never need, and they will ultimately end up taking up space in your home.

Regardless of what you have and don't have, below is a list of a few items you'll absolutely need just to have on hand at all times. Having the right tool can make a difference between a minor inconvenience and a major headache.

- **Hammer**: The old standby. Your trusty sidekick. Whatever you want to call it, very few homes are complete without a decent hammer in the tool belt. Fortunately, a top-of-the-line hammer will only set you back about $30, so you can get one that will last you for years without breaking the bank.

- **Screwdriver**: Ideally, you'll have two different screwdrivers: Phillips and flathead. Honestly, you'll probably end up using the Phillips more often, so if you want to spend a little more on that, go for it. A flat head screwdriver will come in handy to loosen and tighten screws and as a chisel or a wedge, if necessary.

- **Pliers**: Go for the full set on this one—about four or five pliers in all. Try to find a set that includes a needle nose plier, adjustable wrench, slip joint pliers, and maybe even a group joint plier. Some you'll use more than others, but you'll be surprised how often you find yourself reaching for one of these.

- **Measuring tape**: Another extremely inexpensive tool—but one that is absolutely necessary—is a good measuring tape. Look for one that extends to about 8 feet or more, depending on the size of your house. If you're hanging pictures, for example, you'll want to be able to measure the distance of a wall to figure out the halfway point, so find one that has enough length for all your different projects.

- **Level**: It may be tempting to buy a gigantic, 3-foot level that's made of steel and has 14 different markers in it, but really, all you need is one that has two guides—vertical and horizontal. These will come in handy when you hang shelves, build furniture, and even lay flooring.

- **Power drill**: Some may disagree with me here, but having a good, reliable power drill by your side is invaluable. The drill is the one item that you can expect to spend nearly $100 on (or more), and if you take care of it, it can last years. These are useful for drilling pilot holes and doing other large jobs around the house that could take you ten times as long if you try to do them manually.

- **Ladder**: Depending on whether you have a one or two-story house, you'll need a decent ladder to reach light bulbs and hang curtains. Even if you only have a one-story home, try to get a ladder that will reach at least the edge of your house if you need to climb up on your roof. If you are cleaning gutters or doing other roof or overhead work, you will need to include a horizontal support at the top of the ladder and a trustworthy assistant on the ground underneath.

- **Plunger**: A stopped-up toilet isn't that big of a deal, but if you have to head to the store to get a plunger in the middle of a dinner party, it can dampen the mood in a hurry. Not only are these useful for toilets, but you can use them on any pipe, such as a sink, to dislodge a clog quickly. If you have OCD tendencies, you might be inclined to have separate plungers for the toilet and other sinks in the house.

- **Utility knife:** Cutting long strips of just about anything can be tedious but having a solid utility knife can make that job a breeze. You can use it to put marks on woodworking projects, cut rope, and even trim wires if you're especially careful. Like everything else in this list, you'll be surprised how many times it'll save your bacon.

Other guides may add to or take away from this list, but this is a good starting point. Note that I didn't include yard items like a lawnmower or rake, precisely because some homeowners' associations provide these services for you. The tools in this list apply to anyone that calls themself a homeowner but feel free to add to or take away from the list as you see fit.

On the next page, we'll start discussing different scenarios that can happen in your home, and you'll see references to these tools sprinkled throughout. While the list of responsibilities can seem intimidating, don't forget that owning a home is something you should be proud of. It's yours, for better or worse, and what you get out of it is ultimately dependent on what you put into it.

And, by reading this guide (and others), you'll be much more prepared than most of the people on your block. Who knows, maybe you'll even become your neighborhood's "go-to" person for these types of situations. That might be annoying, but it's better than having to find that person to constantly ask for advice.

Trust me, I speak from experience.

CHAPTER 1:

HOW TO FIX A POWER OUTAGE

Power outages can be scary, mainly because they seem to come straight out of nowhere. One minute you're enjoying a nice dinner with your family, and the next, you're sitting in the dark fumbling around for that spare flashlight that you know you put *somewhere*.

As a side note, it's always a good idea to keep a lantern or flashlight in a specific spot so you can find it when you need it. Don't count on using the flashlight on your cell phone, either; depending on how long the power is out, you may not have enough of a charge to carry you through the end of the blackout, and then, you will also not be able to make phone calls.

The first thing you need to do is figure out the extent of the outage. Your home's energy grid is laid out in different sections, so one room will be on one circuit, whereas another room and its outlets will be on another. If only one part of your house is out, then that means that the outage is contained to just that one area. If the power to the entire house is out, step outside and see if your neighbors are affected as well. If so, then it's usually a blown transformer the city will have to fix. In that case, it's just a waiting game until the power comes back on. Call the power company to let them know about the outage, and sit tight.

If the neighbors have power and you don't, then the situation is a little more daunting. Most likely, one of the lines to your specific house has been cut and will need to be fixed, or a different power company serves your house than your neighbors. This is extremely unlikely if you live in a standard suburban neighborhood of quarter-acre plots that sit next to each other, but this is an entirely feasible option if you live out in the country. Still, your main course of action is to call the power company that services your home and let them know about the outage. The total blackout is not something you can usually fix on your own.

By far, the most likely scenario you will face on a semi-regular basis is that only a certain portion of your house has lost power, such as the living room or the bathroom. From here, it's just a matter of conducting a simple Sherlock Holmes-style investigation. Check near the outlets inside the offending area and look for any black marks that might have appeared next to the lightbulb or power outlet. If you see any, it means one of those outlets has been overloaded, and the black mark is a burnt mark that a power surge has left.

Usually, this happens because something has been plugged in that has overloaded the circuit, or a bulb has been installed in a place requiring a higher wattage. The reason your power is out is as a safety mechanism. Instead of setting your house on fire, the power simply shut off instantaneously. Unplug any devices you may have plugged into your wall, and then head to the breaker box that is usually inside your garage, basement, or in an interior closet somewhere.

Crack open the lid of the breaker box and look for any switches that have been flipped. If your home builder was thoughtful (and they should have been, **by law**), every one of the switches will be labeled to designate to which part of the house the power runs. You should notice that the room with lost power has a switch going the opposite direction from the rest of the switches. Simply flip the switch back on, then head back inside your house.

If the power has been restored, then start re-plugging in your devices one by one and turning them on. If the power goes out again, then you know that you're simply overloading the circuit and causing the power to shut off. Unplug the devices again and re-flip the breaker switch.

At this point, you have one of two options. You can either reduce the usage in that room by keeping more of your devices unplugged, or you can call your power company and have them rewire and upgrade your electrical system. The former is easier, but the latter is more effective, especially if the room is a high-usage room, such as an office or a media room. This problem may also affect your resale value, as potential buyers may be scared off by a room that is underdeveloped.

What you do is completely your call, and we recommend keeping only the essential devices plugged in for the short term. If a switch keeps flipping back off, be careful not to keep turning it back on over and over again, as this could potentially cause a short that would result in a fire. If it keeps tripping even after all the devices are unplugged, contact your electrical company to inspect it. You may also have loose wiring somewhere, which is a real danger and needs to be fixed as soon as possible. It may go without saying, but if you see smoke in your house, contact the power company or the fire department immediately. You'd be surprised how many people don't.

CHAPTER 2:

HOW TO PREVENT APPLIANCE FAILURE

As a homeowner, nothing is more fun than getting to play with new appliances? Okay, you don't necessarily have to agree with that statement, but there's no denying the rush you get when you replace your existing *clackety-clank* dishwasher with one that is virtually silent. So much adrenaline. So much excitement.

Still just me? Fine.

Either way, there's no debating the fact that your appliances are an integral part of your lifestyle, so ensuring they stay as efficient as possible should be high on your priority list. Unfortunately, many people think appliances are just "set it and forget it" type fixtures and that as long as it's not broken, everything is fine.

In fact, your appliances can run inefficiently for months or even years before they break down completely, costing you hundreds if not thousands of dollars in higher energy bills, repair jobs, and decreased efficiency along the way. Ensuring they stay operational and avoiding a complete meltdown requires regular maintenance, which, though tedious, should never be overlooked.

Before we talk about how to avoid appliance failure, we should talk for a brief second about what type of appliances to look for in the first place. Like everything else in your home, technology is advancing at a rapid pace, which means the appliances you can choose from today are exponentially better than they were even five years ago. Still, it would be best if you looked for energy-efficient devices. To do that, look for Energy Star approved appliances. These units meet government regulations for higher efficiency and lower carbon footprints. Even if being environmentally friendly aside, you'll still notice the difference in your bank account.

The next question is when to buy your appliances. The average cost of appliances is increasing every year. Refrigerators and dishwashers cost, on average, 5 to 10% more this year than they did last year, regardless of when you're reading this book. To get the most bang for your buck, try to buy your appliances during holiday weekends, such as the Fourth of July or Labor Day, or during the fall, right before new models are released. If you can score a unit straight off of a scratch and dent sale, where there is rarely even a scratch or a dent to begin with, you'll be doing even better. With enough work, true bargains can be found, even when you're dealing with high-priced appliances.

Now, how do you protect these investments? The first thing you need to do is to remember load capacity. There are weight or load limits on these devices for a reason. If you continually jam more clothes in your washer or dryer than it specifies, the belts and the motors on the inside of your units will depreciate rapidly, forcing you to buy a new one prematurely.

Moreover, you'll notice your clothes aren't as clean as they could be, simply because there's not enough movement and space for the cleaning agents to reach all parts of the garments. I know it's hard but **resist** the temptation to stuff as much as you can inside your appliances.

Secondly, make sure you clean them regularly. Cleaning is easy to do when you're talking about a dishwasher, where food particles are easily scooped off the bottom of the unit. But, it becomes a little more laborious when you're thinking about cleaning the coils on the back of your refrigerator. You don't have to do this often, but every six months or so, pull your refrigerator out, get behind it, and wipe down the coils with a rag. Doing so will ensure you don't have freezing problems or ice buildup, which can clog your water and cause a flood in your kitchen.

Likewise, you should always try to keep water away from electrical parts as much as possible. Not only could you short out your unit, but you can also create a safety hazard. To be safe, whenever you decide to work on your unit, unplug it to kill the current. The last thing you want is to be electrocuted by a garbage disposal!

While you're behind the refrigerator and inspecting other various appliances, it's a good idea to tighten up any loose bolts you may see hanging around. Normally, these are fastened so tightly during the installation process that it's a bigger concern to try and get them off than it is to keep them tight, but that doesn't mean they won't come undone over time. A simple hand tighten should do the trick.

One of the biggest areas mostly neglected by homeowners is maintaining a dryer properly. Most people know that you should scrape the lint trap inside your dryer every single time you put new clothes in it, but few are aware of the dangers that come from not cleaning out your exhaust pipe. That tube that comes from behind the dryer and spits hot air into the atmosphere can be a magnet for dust, dirt, and lint and should be cleaned every six months, at least. Most hardware stores sell a simple brush you can attach to the end of a power drill to force lint from the pipe's top, or you can also schedule a dryer exhaust pipe cleaning as part of your yearly tune-up.

Speaking of tune-ups, make sure you schedule them. Your HVAC system, your plumbing system, and your electrical system could each use yearly tune-ups to ensure they are working properly. Try to schedule them during the off-season to save a little bit of money. The transition zone between spring and summer is usually a slow time for HVAC companies. Even though these tune-ups may set you back a few hundred dollars every year, they'll save you thousands over the life of your home in terms of energy costs and preventive maintenance. More than one homeowner has turned on their furnace at the beginning of winter only to find the unit has stopped working over the course of the year. A maintenance contract will ensure that that's not you, which would — quite literally — leave you out in the cold.

CHAPTER 3:

HOW TO KEEP YOUR HOME FROM BURNING DOWN

I recognize a strong case to be made for this chapter appearing first in this book, but hopefully, placing it this early means it will still be read with some regularity.

I also recognize that this is, perhaps, the number one fear of many first-time homeowners. I remember my hesitation when I accepted the keys to my first house, then walked in and thought about all the wires that ran through it, praying one of them wouldn't unintentionally spark and burn the entire place to the ground.

Fortunately, house fires are relatively rare, and the ones that do take place very rarely engulf the entire structure. Sometimes they go out by themselves, but most often, a quick response and knowing a few basic skills will help to prevent the unthinkable from happening. Moreover, basic prevention tips will help keep the entire event from happening in the first place.

Rather than bore you with multiple paragraphs of information to digest and think about, I've installed a list of tips to memorize for this chapter. It's unlikely you'll keep them all at the ready 100% of the time, but there are some common themes throughout that should help you recognize danger when you see it.

1. **Install smoke alarms.** This is a no-brainer. The National Fire Protection Association recommends one fire alarm for every bedroom inside your house, one outside every sleeping area, and one on every floor of your house. If you have a two-story house plus a basement, that makes three smoke alarms on every level, at least. If you have five bedrooms, then that adds up to eight and probably three outside of the three sleeping areas, making eleven. That may sound like a lot, but fortunately, fire alarms are relatively inexpensive

and easy to maintain. Besides replacing the batteries when they go out, the only thing you need to do after installing them is to test them every six months. To do that, press and hold the test button on the smoke detector and wait for a high-pitched squeal. If you hear it, it's still operational.

2. **Buy a fire extinguisher.** Since fires can happen at any time, in any place, for any reason, you'll need an easily accessible fire extinguisher on every floor of your home. You should also familiarize yourself with how to use it, or else you'll be trying to read the instructions in the middle of a panic. If that's not a recipe for disaster, I don't know what is.

3. **Never leave a flame unattended.** On average, nearly 180,000 fires in the United States are related to cooking, while candles cause another 8000. The best course of action, then, is to never leave an open flame unattended for any length of time, but especially not one that has the

potential to spread in a hurry. Grease fires, caused when grease splashes out of the pan and ignites instantly, are one of the most dangerous since water actually *spreads* the fire instead of putting it out. If one starts, try to cover it with a metal lid if you can, and cover the flame in baking soda.

4. **Know your wattage.** More than one fire has been caused by a lightbulb that was not rated for the amount of electricity that courses through it. When it explodes, it will not only send shrapnel nearby but also could start a fire. If you're unsure about the wattage, simply touch near where the bulb is connected (but not inside the socket) and see if it feels hot. If so, replace the bulb. The same can apply to anything that's plugged into an outlet, too. If there's heat near the outlet, unplug it immediately.

5. **Clean your chimney**. Modern chimneys are remarkably efficient, but that doesn't mean they don't need to be cleaned out every once in a while.

If you're somebody who uses your fireplace often, then you most likely have a layer of creosote built up on the inside of your exhaust. This is extremely flammable, but it can also attract birds and rodents, building their nests inside the chimney. At that point, you not only have a blockage that can send smoke billowing back inside your house but also something potentially flammable that can light up your roof.

6. **Have your electrical system inspected.** Although it might be impossible for you to inspect every single wire in your house, an electrician has the training and tools necessary to get the job done. If they spot a frayed wire, they'll be able to replace it before it causes an issue, no matter how big. This becomes even more important with older homes, as outdated wiring and fuse boxes have a higher potential for shorts. It will be frustrating to replace the wiring in your house, but it's much better than the alternative.

7. **Be careful with space heaters**. Many people love a space heater inside their office or bedroom to provide warmth so they don't have to heat their entire home, which can be expensive. There's nothing wrong with that, but be careful about what you put your space heater next to. The coils on the back of the space heater, for instance, can get especially hot and start a fire with a nearby blanket. Furthermore, if you plan on plugging the heater into a surge protector, make sure the surge protector is rated high enough. Or, better yet, plug directly into the wall instead.

CHAPTER 4:

HOW TO DEFEND YOUR CASTLE (FROM HUMANS)

When it comes to home defense systems, there are two options. First, you can ignore defense completely and hope you never have a burglar show up at your house, or you can go full-on Rambo and turn your home into an absolute fortress, complete with bungee pits, booby-traps, and a .50 caliber turret mounted on the top of your house.

Unfortunately, your local HOA (or just your average neighbors) won't be too keen on the idea of having explosives going off at all hours of the night, so ideally, you should find somewhere in the middle of those two extremes to settle. But even if you're not importing weapons off the black market to defend your home, you can still have a sizable defense system.

The only thing you really need to have is a plan. Understanding the neighborhood you live in, as well as the particular risks associated with your house, can answer a lot of questions. If you live in a quiet cul-de-sac at the end of a deep residential neighborhood, for instance, your chances of being burglarized diminish greatly. Remember, thieves like to be in and out with as little fuss as possible, so the primary objective is to make your house less appealing than everybody else's.

Conversely, if you live in the middle of nowhere, with dozens of acres surrounding you and the house next to you, you need to be more aware of your environment. Treelines that are close to your house can be havens for thieves to get up next to you and pounce when you least expect it. Rather than treat this as a constant sense of paranoia, treat it as a puzzle that needs to be solved.

Even if you never invest in a security system, there are several things you can do right off the bat to make your home less appealing. Adding a sticker from an alarm company can deter some thieves, as can putting a door brace behind your entryway door, securing your sliding doors, and shutting your blinds at night. You'd be surprised how many burglars are brazen enough to walk right up to your window, peek inside, and plan what their next move will be right at the moment.

Technology has made home security almost a joy to invest in. Smart locks, security cameras, and motion sensors are at your disposal and can now be bought at a relatively affordable price. If you wanted to deck out your home 30 years ago, you needed to schedule an appointment with a security advisor who would walk through your home with you and identify weak points. Then, they would hardwire cameras throughout your house — which almost always looked terrible — then run them all to a main central display inside a closet. It was a monumental effort that usually required a minor construction project to accomplish.

Now, you can outfit your home with better technology in a couple of hours for less than $500 — all in. Most of this hardware can be bought online or at your local hardware store, and there are numerous tutorials on how to install it yourself. Best of all, mobile apps allow you to monitor your house even when you're away.

I'm a big proponent of smart-home technology, but inevitably, people ask me whether or not putting your home on a "smart security network" poses additional risks by hackers. There is a good argument to be made for this, but in my experience, the type of thieves who sit outside your home and tap into your network are not average run-of-the-mill thieves you need to be worried about. *Every day*, 4,800 burglaries happen in the United States, and the average property loss is less than $3000. No thief will invest in months of technological education and thousands of dollars worth of equipment to steal that "little" amount of money.

Instead, I always encourage people to focus on the basics. A security camera above doors, driveways, and your yard should be enough, but if you have a second floor or basement, consider putting a camera in those locations as well. There's no need to place them in bedrooms or bathrooms and be careful about pointing them toward your neighbor's property, as that may be illegal in certain states. Set cameras high enough that you have a good vantage point for possible intruders, and also be sure to avoid any blind spots. Even petty thieves are good at spotting the best place to hide from a camera, whether it's in the bushes or around the corner of your house.

Moving inside your home, you should put a window sensor on every window of your house. These usually are magnetic strips that sound an alarm when the window is separated (assuming that it's armed) and can provide a major deterrent for burglars. Glass break sensors are another great addition to your home — usually two will suffice — as are motion sensors in the main living areas. The difference between these and your cameras is that sensors don't record anything that's taking place; they just track motion as it passes through your house. An unfortunate side effect is that if you decide to get up in the middle of the night for a drink of water, you may notice a brief light as the sensor attacks your presence. Try not to stare directly into it. Another downside is that sensors don't detect the difference between humans and house pets that like to roam at night.

If you decide to get a home security system — and I strongly encourage you to do so — you'll need to register it with your municipality. Although first responders will come to any home in the event of an emergency, if you don't have an alarm permit set up, you could face a sizeable fine after it's all over. The rates on these permits vary from city to city, but they're usually less than $100 a year.

Another cost to be aware of is the cost of monitoring your system. Most home security companies will package their setups in two ways: DIY or professional installation. DIY is more expensive initially, but you also own the equipment and can move it from place to place. Professional installs are usually free, but you'll have a monthly cost associated. I recommend shelling out for a DIY install to upgrade and customize to your liking and pay a much lower monthly rate for professional monitoring. Still, even with everything we've discussed so far, you shouldn't be out more than $1000 for a robust security system, alarm permits, and one year of monitoring. Not a bad investment, considering what it is you're protecting.

One final note about home security. You may not realize it, but one of the best things you can invest in to protect your home can also become your best friend: dogs. These four-legged friends instinctively protect not only their owners but also their property (they learn very quickly where their home is) and act as a mobile police force for your home. While big dogs like German shepherds may be your first thought (and are usually better), don't discount smaller dogs that have a quick bite and a big bark. In one survey of ex-thieves, they admitted dogs were more likely to scare them off than anything else, except video cameras. So, if you don't want to invest in a security system and prefer to have a friend do all your work for you, you can't go wrong with a dog. Plus, you get all the snuggles too! It's a win-win.

CHAPTER 5:

HOW TO DEFEND YOUR CASTLE (FROM PESTS)

Thieves that might break into your house during a warm summer day are not the only threats you need to be aware of. Pest control is also a big deal and can turn your home from a comfortable oasis into a putrid nightmare in a hurry. Few things are less appetizing than getting dinner prepared on your kitchen counter, only to notice a trail of ants carrying part of your dessert away.

Just like home security systems, though, pest control can be done by yourself. You can take several different approaches to eliminate pests from your house, many of which revolve around simply maintaining proper hygiene. That's not to say that anybody who reads this is inherently dirty, but it's a good idea to take a few extra preventative steps to ensure that your home is free from anything that might make it appealing to pests. Sugar, crumbs, and even dirt left out on a countertop or floor are magnets for pests and should be cleaned up as soon as possible.

The quickest and easiest route for pest control is to hire the labor out. This is still the most popular choice for homeowners, as the different types of pests you may deal with will change from place to place. A home based in rural Arkansas, for instance, will face different challenges than an apartment in downtown Seattle.

Unfortunately, professional pesticide services can be expensive. If you go for a full treatment, you should expect to pay around $200 every three months to have a technician come out and spray your home (depending on what type of services you hire). The chemicals they use these days are not nearly as harmful as they used to be, but you still may have to vacate your house for an hour or so, or at the very least, keep your kids and pets away from areas that have been directly sprayed.

The plus side of professional pest control is that they have unique concoctions and chemical agents that are not always available to homeowners and, more importantly, know how to mix them to prevent bugs from ever even appearing inside your home or yard. I still remember one occasion where I found a few colonies of bees inside the tree in our front yard. I called our pest control guy and watched as he sprayed some kind of orange and pink fog into the tree. I watched as dozens of bees dropped out of the sky like raindrops. That's not something I would've been able to take care of by myself.

The ability to automate your pest control services is very appealing to many busy families, so it's not a solution that should be directly overlooked. If you *do* decide to go the DIY route, know that you'll be in for an uphill battle at the beginning. Termite traps that are placed, for example, may not get rid of the original infestation but *can* deter termites from building a colony months down the road. It's a marathon, not a sprint, so don't forget to be patient.

You should also be very careful with what you're doing. Homemade pest killers are safer than they used to be, but that's not to say that they won't hurt a child or a pet if they're ingested. Keep them out of sight if at all possible and use them as minimally as possible. One other alternative is to create a homemade solution you can spray every so often as a regular deterrent. Just take a 16-ounce spray bottle, fill it with 14 ounces of distilled water, and put in a few drops of lavender and eucalyptus essential oils. Although it's not bulletproof, it can provide a layer of protection against some of the most common bugs you may find, such as beetles, fleas, lice, and moths.

By far, it's easier to keep pests out of your house in the first place than try to get rid of them once they're already inside (the same is true of burglars, now that I think about it). Prevention is the key here, and establishing good habits is paramount to making sure this is a battle you don't have to fight nearly as often. Below is a list of a few bullet points to keep in mind.

Read through them a few times, but eventually, they'll become second nature.

- **Keep food tucked away.** Anything left on the counter can attract pests, including mice, so make sure you put all your food away as soon as you're done and clean up the area once you're finished.

- **Keep your home dry.** Mosquitoes and other pests love standing water, so if you have a drip underneath your faucet or a puddle outside, you can almost guarantee there will be bugs nearby too. Keep areas dry, and that'll keep you out of a lot of trouble.

- **Clean up your clutter.** Contrary to popular belief, bugs do not generally "attack" humans. Most of them prefer to stay out of sight as much as possible and only react when entering their area. One of spiders' favorite homes, for example, is a pile of clothes or toys in a corner. They'll get in there, spin their web, and mostly become dormant, but once that area is disturbed, they could become very active. Minimize the risk by cleaning up your clutter.

- **Move firewood** away from home. This is probably one of the most common and easiest mistakes to make as a homeowner. Firewood stacked inside the house or up against the home on the outside is a prime location for termites to use as a launching point to invade your home. They can sit right next to your house and eat away at your framing for months—or even years—before you realize it. Find a new home for firewood, and you shouldn't have that issue.

If you have any questions, it never hurts to hire a professional pest control service to come out and do an initial evaluation of your home and alert you to possible pests. Once you're familiar with the type of threats unique to your area, you can draft a strategy and set up a schedule. Success may not come overnight, but this is one of those areas where you can take a lot of pride in protecting your castle, as you dutifully repel the threats — both big and small — that can threaten your home.

CHAPTER 6:

HOW TO SAVE ON ENERGY COSTS

When it comes to expenses inside your home, few can add up quicker than your energy bills. If you or your family enjoy your house particularly hot or cold, then you can expect to spend a substantial amount of your income every month on energy bills. Ideally, though, your utility cost should be no more than 8 to 10% of your monthly income, so try whatever you can to get within that range, and your budget should be fine.

But what are you supposed to do if your energy costs skyrocket? If you notice an immediate increase in a bill such as water or electricity, look for the source for starters. A water leak is very possible, as is a fan that has been shifted from "auto" to "on" mode and is constantly running. Even if those do happen, you shouldn't notice your bill rising more than a few hundred dollars, unless it's a *major* leak. If you see a huge jump in your bill, contact your utility department. It may be that they simply read the meter wrong, which happens more than you would think.

Barring an emergency situation, how do you routinely keep your energy bills lower even as they constantly increase year after year? The first thing you should do is have a home energy audit conducted. These can run you a few hundred dollars, but they can also provide remarkable insight into the energy usage in your home. Leaky windows and holes in your ductwork can be subtle but major drains on your utilities, and they usually require a professional HVAC technician to identify and fix.

An auditor will also examine the state of your HVAC system and recommend either a tune-up or replacement. Replacing your HVAC system doesn't sound like fun (and it isn't), but it may be a lifesaver if your system is on the verge of collapsing. An auditor will also spot potential problem areas that can cause your system to work harder than normal. Even if your HVAC system is reliably pumping out hot and cold air, if the parts are worn down, or there's a buildup of grime and dirt on the inside of the system, the motor will run harder and burn more energy. Cleaning it can do wonders.

Once your auditor has conducted a thorough examination of your house and given you a list of things to work through, shift your attention to energy-saving appliances and fixtures. LED light bulbs that last longer and burn easier should provide a boost, as do the Energy-Star rated appliances we mentioned earlier. Smart power strips can be used to connect multiple devices at once, and the temperature in your water heater can be adjusted. This will force your unit not to run as hard, which will save you money in the long run.

There are also lifestyle changes you can make. Taking colder and shorter showers will help ease the pressure on your plumbing system, as will washing your clothes in cold water instead of hot. You can turn your thermostat up or down a degree (depending on the season) and replace your showerhead to a more energy-efficient nozzle.

One smart move that doesn't require a lifestyle change but can significantly impact your budget is to call your utility company and ask for discounted rates or a switch to average rates. Depending on your income level, you may qualify for a lower energy bill that is subsidized by the government or the community. Rebate programs may also be in place from the government if you install certain appliances, so be sure to take advantage of those, too.

Having your home on an average billing cycle instead of a fluctuating cycle will also help make your bills more predictable, and for that reason, is becoming more popular amongst utility companies. Instead of simply charging you for the amount of usage you had that month, which can vary drastically throughout the year, they add up your usage over a series of months and charge you an average rate every month. You'll still see it go up or down, but the change won't nearly be as drastic.

Individually, none of these changes sound like that big of a deal; after all, how does taking a slightly colder shower help put money back in your pocket? Once you add them all together, though, you could be looking at a substantial decrease in your energy bills every year, as well as decreased wear and tear on your units, which means they'll last longer. Ignore them at your peril, but if you put awareness off for too long, you could be staring at a bill for a complete HVAC and plumbing replacement, which will stretch into several thousand dollars and beyond.

CHAPTER 7:

HOW TO WIN
THE YARD WARS

Finally, my favorite chapter of the book! I absolutely love lawn care and everything that goes along with it, including fertilizing, mowing, edging, and yes, even laying down weedkiller. There are few things I enjoy more about owning my own home than having a nice, lush yard that is the envy of everybody in the neighborhood. Those stares your neighbors give your yard when they walk by and the subtle compliments they offer—even to themselves—make it all worth it.

I'll admit though, I wasn't always built this way. Growing up, I had a yard business to help pay for my first car, but it was always drudgery to push the mower down the block and mow my neighbors' yards. I hated the dust that kicked up and the sun beating down all day, but as an adult, I love it because I know I'm taking care of *my* yard, not somebody else's. Having ownership of your own little patch of land and cultivating it is, to me, one of the purest responsibilities we have as human beings. I feel a responsibility to not just make my yard beautiful but also healthy in the process.

Granted, this will take a little bit more commitment from you as the homeowner, but the good news is that, in this situation, an ounce of prevention is worth 100 pounds of cure. Most people pay very little attention to the yard outside of mowing it when the weeds get high, but by having a steady routine of watering and fertilizing, you'll be able to make your yard stand apart in the crowd.

First, though, I need to make a quick caveat. There is no way I can cover everything that goes into making a perfect yard in this short chapter. This is designed to be a primer, something to wet your whistle and spur you on to invest in other resources. There are a number of different professionals out there that will provide tips on DIY lawn care, so the best thing you can do is find one that specializes in either northern or southern lawns (depending on where you live) and learn as much as you can.

Be wary, though, that this will be a slow burn. You most likely won't notice the effects overnight, but given enough time, you'll start to see results. My goal, as a homeowner, was to have my yard comfortable enough so my family could walk around on it without shoes. Accomplishing that goal is a pretty big deal for me, and I'm sure it will be for you too.

Let's start at the beginning, with the most basic tool you'll need — a lawnmower. Even if you don't care about your yard (how could you!), you'll still be expected by your neighbors to keep your lawn looking somewhat presentable. You can get a lawnmower from your local hardware store for a few hundred bucks, but if you have more than about 20,000 ft.^{2}, I would recommend getting a riding lawnmower or a zero-turn. Not only is the wheelbase larger so you can cover more ground, but it's more comfortable to ride than walk.

Mowing an acre of grass with a push mower could take hours, which is a lot, no matter how much you love yard work.

There are also manual reel mowers that can be had for less than $100 and are perfect if you're looking to create a golf course feel for your Bermuda grass. The downside to these, though, is that they usually require more maintenance than other mowers because you have to keep the blades extra sharp. Furthermore, if you have tall grass, reel mowers are not really very effective, and in some cases, they won't work at all. They may not require gas or oil, and the mulching goes straight back into the yard, which helps create a healthier yard, but you'll have to do your own cost/benefit analysis to decide what's right for you.

Next, let's talk about irrigation. Tractor sprinklers are fine, but you have to monitor them and move them throughout the day, which makes it hard for people who work outside the home. An irrigation system can be scheduled for any time of the day or week, but they can be expensive to install; an average professional set will set you back close to $5000, or you can DIY it for around $1000.

The trick to irrigation is knowing when to water your yard. Ideally, you would have your entire yard watered sometime in the very early morning hours, around 4 or 5 AM. This allows the water enough time actually to get into your soil; wait too long, and the heat of the day will burn it off, while any earlier will cause the water to develop a fungus in your yard possibly. Aim to water your yard around one to two times a week, and you should be fine.

Weed killer will also be an essential part of your arsenal, so head down to your hardware store and look for one that offers a blanket application and kills many different weeds. You can always go back later and get a weed killer that targets specific weeds, such as dandelions or clovers, but most people don't bother. One- or two-yearly blanket applications of weedkiller, or post-emergent, as it's called, should help tremendously. You can also put down a layer of pre-emergent in the early spring and late fall to help neutralize weeds from even appearing in the first place.

As for fertilizer, you'll want to put that down three to four times throughout the year—about every 6 to eight weeks or so. Go with organic fertilizer if you can, since that won't "burn" the yard, but as long as you follow the application instructions on the package, everything will be okay.

As I said earlier, you can take care of your yard in many different ways, and this short chapter is meant to introduce the topic. You're free to skip over this chapter if you want, but I would encourage you to at least follow the basic instructions presented here so your yard looks presentable. Your neighbors will certainly appreciate it, and the entire community will benefit since good-looking yards eventually help with resale value. You don't want to be that one house in the neighborhood people hold their nose at as they drive by, so having a little bit of pride in your property will make all the difference.

CHAPTER 8:

SEVEN PRINCIPLES FOR LANDSCAPING SUCCESS

I hope this doesn't work against me, but as fanatical as I am about yard care, I don't enjoy landscaping that much. That's because, unlike my wife, I don't have quite the eye for design that true landscaping mastery requires. So, I struggle to know what looks good, what goes where, and what flowers to mix with which other plants.

To help with that, I rely on a few basic principles to make sure my landscaping looks *solid*, rather than "blow-everyone-out-of-the-water" amazing, like some people. Can I hire a professional to come in and design it all for me? Sure, but that's not my style. I'm DIY all the way and always recommend that for first-time homeowners. There is no better way to learn about your house than by trying to do as much as you can by yourself first. You may be different, and that's fine. Still, it never hurts to understand a few basic principles when it comes to landscaping design.

These are the ideas that I cling to—the ones that have helped me the most over the years. When in doubt, stick to them also, and you'll be a lot better off than most.

Start Small

Far too many homeowners wake up on a Saturday morning, tune in to HGTV, and immediately start plotting ideas of what they want their dream house to look like. Before long, they're off to the local hardware store, where they spend nearly $1000 on tools and resources, with only the visions in their head to guide them.

This is almost certainly a recipe for disaster. Instead of redoing your entire flower bed from top to bottom, start small by experimenting with few flowers here and there. Even better, instead of going straight for the beautiful roses, you see on someone else's driveway, first, figure out which kind of flower looks best in your yard. Then, design the edging that will help your garden pop. Work forward from there.

Above all else, take your time. Plants don't grow overnight, and the best yards in the neighborhood are not the ones that are hastily thrown together on a Saturday before Little League. Instead, they're usually the result of a well-thought-out and crafted plan that started with one person being curious about how to make a tiny portion of their flower bed look better. Start small and look at it as a marathon instead of a sprint.

Find Your Focus

For some people, a lovely birdbath is the centerpiece of their garden. Others may be more drawn to a tall plant that towers over the neighboring windows. Whatever your focal point is, build around that instead of throwing a bunch of major set pieces together and hoping something beautiful comes out.

This is all part of starting small and then growing from there, as it will allow you to take a step back and design your yard visually, rather than from a dream board on Pinterest. You'll also get a good idea of the style of your yard, whether or not certain bushes would cause the slope in your yard to appear too drastic, for example. Regardless, start with a single piece of architecture or a single plant and build out from there.

Understand Your Needs

Landscaping is a very personal endeavor. Some people love a flower garden that has every different type of plant under the sun, while others enjoy a lush garden of potatoes and squash in their backyard. Every person is different, so every landscaping need is different as well. Knowing what you and your family want will very quickly define what you decide to do.

Furthermore, knowing what type of plants you want will dictate what kind of beds you erect in the first place. Raised flower beds, irrigation systems, and the location of your plants will all come into view depending on what you decide to put in. Whether you want it to be beautiful or utilitarian, or both, take stock of what you want and need to do and decide what is most important at this point in your life.

Pivot, If Necessary

Undoubtedly, once you begin your landscaping project, there'll be things you love and things you hate. Maybe it's that plant that you spent $40 on that just looks horrid next to a $6 plant you got from the discount aisle at a department store. Or maybe it's the fact that your flower bed is much too large for the plants you put in, or that the rocks you spread out don't trap in moisture nearly as well as mulch. It doesn't matter what the problem is—staying true to a design even when you know it's faulty is a surefire way to hate your garden. If you notice something that's out of place, don't be afraid to swap it for something completely different.

Location, Location, Location

Not every part of your yard was created equal. Some will have shade, while others will have a significant amount of sun, and knowing what plants do better in what places can make all the difference in the world. Some plants need only a few hours of direct sunlight, while some need as much as possible. If you swap the two, you're almost guaranteed to have plants that will underperform and look squatty when compared to their full-grown counterparts.

Study your yard to find out which areas get the most sun and pick the most appropriate place. You can do a lot of online research to help with this, or you can talk to somebody at your local nursery to help design your flower bed for you. They interact with many people who have different projects daily, so they're well-equipped to offer this kind of guidance.

Don't Forget About Irrigation

All those plants you put in will need something to keep them alive, and typical tractor waterers usually won't work as well in your garden as they do on your lawn. You'll need to install something that can be done either in tandem with your home's irrigation system, or you'll need to schedule a time to go out there with the water hose and spray them all down. For some people, this is very therapeutic; indeed, it is pretty soothing to stand out in your yard on a cool summer night and hose down some plants. I've tried it several times for different reasons, and it is relaxing.

But it's also easy to forget to do, and if you fail to irrigate your plants properly, you'll end up with an entire yard full of weeds and dead plants, which will make your garden look even worse than it did at the beginning. Don't let all that hard work go to waste by allowing your plants to die — set up something simple that you can manage, have a schedule, and stick to it.

Enjoy Your Work

I cannot stress this enough: if you don't enjoy your yard, you won't maintain it. So many people set off in the morning to create a beautiful landscape piece when they have absolutely no intention of enjoying it themselves. Instead, they're doing it to keep up with their neighbors, or they want to maximize the resale value through curb appeal. Landscaping is meant to be enjoyed; I'm a big fan of creating a sitting space somewhere near your flowerbeds so that you can do precisely *that*. A bench or even a chair that you can spend time in will help you fully appreciate all the work you've done.

Even the process of working in the garden can be wonderful. I have a neighbor who spends most of her Saturday mornings weeding the garden and moving things around, all while blasting 90s hip-hop in her driveway. I used to find it annoying, but now I envy it. She has something stable that she can work on every single week, an anchor by which she can enjoy her home. Her gratification comes when so much of homeownership is utilitarian in nature, keeping us warm and safe, giving us a place to sleep, etc. — having a garden she can truly enjoy provides a wonderful escape to the hustle and bustle of everyday life.

CHAPTER 9:

HOW TO PAINT LIKE A PRO

From my most favorite to my least favorite subject — as much as I enjoy lawn care, painting has always filled me with a sense of dread. I don't know why since many people enjoy it, but it's just one of those things I always try to avoid if at all possible.

With that in mind, the first piece of information I can give you is that if you can afford to hire this part of your life out, I would do it in a heartbeat. The problem with painting is not just that it's difficult but that it's time intensive and difficult to get right. Even if you can get the right color combinations to match the right texture, you still have to move all the furniture around, cover the floors, and go over the area about two or three times to get it to look good.

For many people, this process is therapeutic. For me, I just grit my teeth and try to survive.

If you are determined to paint your house yourself, you'll need a few pieces of equipment to make the job a little easier. Whether you want to paint inside or outside, you'll need a paint brush, painter's tape, drop cloths, and plastic sheeting. If you're painting a tall wall or outside your home, you'll also need a ladder.

The inside and outside of your home will require paint and primer (look closely at the label to see if it's interior or exterior, depending on your project); the primer will go on first and provide a base layer while the paint provides aesthetic appeal. If you're painting the exterior of your house, you'll also need to grab a pressure washer, paint scraper, epoxy filler, spackle knife, caulk, and caulk gun.

People paint the inside or outside of their home for different reasons. Some people want to make their house stand out and drive higher resale value, while others simply want to repair damage that has taken place. Additionally, a solid paint job can actually *protect* your home from rain and sunshine, which wear down the exterior of the house over time.

Let's start with the outside first. No matter your reason for painting your home's exterior, the first thing you need to do is blast it with your pressure washer to remove all the dirt and debris that has collected over time. Absolutely nothing looks worse on a home than a paint job with dirt and hair trapped inside it. Even worse, debris is almost impossible to get out. Blast the dirt off first, then inspect the walls for any kind of damage. Chips, cracks, or holes need to be filled with epoxy filler and scraped with a spackle knife to smooth over.

Once you've done that, take your paint scraper and remove any loose chips of paint you see and sand these areas down. Put an extra layer of caulk on the seams of the windows to provide insulation and keep paint from coming inside the home, wrap any exterior fixtures, put a sheet up against the house to protect the grass, and, finally, lay down a thick coat of exterior paint. Don't be surprised if you have to go back over the area a couple of times to get it right. Exterior surfaces are notorious for not holding paint very well. It's how they also protect your home from rainwater and debris.

If you need to paint the inside of your house, the job is slightly easier in terms of effort but more complex because it requires a little bit more finesse. You'll still want to wipe down the surface to get all dirt and debris off and fix any damages to the wall, but you'll also want to remove the faceplates of light switches and outlets and cover any exposed outlets as well. Then, tape the borders of the wall to create a fine edge along where you're painting, cover the carpet with a tarp, and put your primer down. In some cases, you may be able to buy a primer and paint combo though these seldom work as well as separating the two (just like those shampoo and conditioner hybrids). Still, they can work great in a pinch or for a small area.

Then, get out your regular paint and go to town. To cover large areas, I suggest using a paint sprayer (if you have one) or, at the very least, a paint roller. You'll need a tray into which to pour the paint, but if you have a good roller, you should be able to cover quite a bit of area in a very short amount of time. Use a fine paintbrush to get along the wall's edges and leave the paint to dry before deciding on a second or third coat.

Painting the inside of your home involves quality more than quantity. You can get cheap paintbrushes and equipment for not very much money, but you'll also be making your work ten times harder than it needs to be. In fact, and this is a theme that will run throughout most of the adventures you have as a homeowner, when you can, always invest in quality. It may be more expensive initially, but it will save you from having to run to the store to buy a replacement.

Not to mention: your back will thank you also.

CHAPTER 10:

HOW TO UNCLOG
A TOILET

This will be a short chapter, and you may be wondering why I'm devoting an entire section to simply unclogging your toilet. The truth is: this is one of those activities that can dramatically change your day. One second, you're in the middle of a dinner party, and the next, you have a guest whispering in your ear that sewage is spilling into your floor and needs to be taken care of *NOW*.

So, what you do? The first thing is to evaluate the situation. If water is running constantly, you need to find a way to shut it off. Nearly every toilet on the market today is equipped with a shut-off valve directly behind the toilet. Look for it, and either pull or twist the lever to shut the water off. If that's not turning off, then you may need to go outside and shut the main water valve off, although that would be a more extreme measure. Not only will your toilet stop running, but every other waterline in the house will shut off as well. You don't want to keep the main water line off for too long, as running water helps keep clogs from occurring.

Next, look in the toilet and see if you can identify the cause of the problem. If the clog is only happening to one toilet, the problem is isolated to this toilet. Grab a plunger and start thrusting up and down semi-rapidly, creating suction, to see if you can dislodge the clog. Most of the time, the clog will simply slide down the pipe and into the main sewer line, and you'll be good to go. Alternatively, you can use a metal hanger or even your fingers, Ugh! to try and dislodge the clog manually but be careful if you have PVC or old copper pipes. You could unintentionally damage the lines if you apply too much pressure.

If none of those approaches work, you still have a few tricks up your sleeve. Grab a pot of hot water (not boiling) and put a few drops of liquid dishwashing soap inside. This will help with lubrication and hopefully allow the clog to slide into the main sewer line, while the hot water should give the debris enough of a shock to dislodge it as well.

Your absolute last course of action is to remove the toilet completely. This isn't a particularly hard job, but it can be messy if you don't approach it the right way. First, remove as much water from the bowl in the tank as you can into a bucket nearby. Then, remove the two bolts on either side of the toilet that are keeping the commode flush against the floor (no pun intended). Lift the toilet up slightly and move it off to the side. You may have some running water that comes out the bottom, so have towels and a garbage bag ready just in case.

From here, the main water line should be exposed. You may be able to notice the clog sitting up at the top; if so, simply grab it and reattach the toilet. If not, try to look inside the toilet pipes to see if you can remove the clog that way. If the obstacle is not in the toilet and you can't see it from the main water line, then your only option left is to call a plumber and have them dislodge it professionally. Of all the possible plumbing fixes you could have, this is by far the cheapest. That doesn't make it any more exciting, though.

If you have more than one toilet backing up, then the problem isn't located in one pipe but all of them. At this point, you'll definitely need to shut the main water valve off and call a professional plumber — ideally, an emergency plumber. Backed-up water inside your sewer lines can put pressure on the pipes and cause them to crack, possibly causing a spill inside your yard or even in your house. Professional plumbers have the tools to perform fixes such as a trenchless sewer repair, which uses a scope to travel down the pipe and fix the crack from the inside. This is a lot easier (and cheaper) than a traditional sewer line repair, where they have to excavate the entire pipe to fix the leak.

Even though we've been talking about a single toilet backing up, it's worth mentioning that the same fixes can apply to any pipes in your house, such as sinks or shower drains. Over-the-counter chemical solutions are not necessarily evil, but if used too much, they can erode your pipes from the inside out, so use them sparingly. Always look for DIY or manual techniques first, but don't hesitate to call a plumber if the job appears to be too big. If you don't, you may end up paying not only for the fix but for a repair job as well.

CHAPTER 11:

HOW TO KEEP YOUR HOME'S HVAC SYSTEM RUNNING EFFICIENTLY

Even if you don't know what an HVAC system is, I guarantee you're familiar with what it does. HVAC stands for heating, ventilation, and air conditioning, which means it's responsible for directing, regulating, and maintaining the temperature and airflow throughout your entire home. Sound complicated? Don't worry, it's not nearly as intense as you may think.

Fortunately, the HVAC systems installed in just about every modern home on the planet are energy-efficient and easy to handle for even the busiest of homeowners. Replacing a couple of filters a few times a year and making sure all the vents are free from obstructions will likely be the most maintenance you'll ever need to do, apart from scheduling a routine inspection. If you don't want to do even that, most HVAC companies also offer a home maintenance plan that can allow you to take a fully hands-off approach to your home's airflow.

Whether you hire it out or do it yourself, the fact remains that your HVAC needs to be taken care of. Just like with your plumbing and electrical systems, any small issues left for a long period of time can create much larger problems down the road. Over time, your unit will work harder and harder to cool and heat the same amount of air in your home, which will drive your energy bills sky high. You'll also notice a rapid deterioration of your unit, which will require frequent repairs and possible premature replacement. When you consider the fact that a full HVAC system replacement starts at around $5,000, you realize just how much financial sense it makes to take 10 minutes of your time every couple of months to check on your HVAC system.

But first, a word of warning. Even though your unit is less complex than it was 50 years ago, that doesn't mean that you should try to work on it yourself. The air ducts that travel through your house snake over beams in the ceiling and across flimsy sheetrock; one wrong step and you can find yourself falling two stories down to your living room couch and then to the hospital. It's tempting to perform even simple maintenance on your unit yourself, but if there's any doubt *at all*, hire it out.

Working on your actual air conditioning and heating units is even more of a challenge. These devices can weigh a few hundred pounds at the lightest and require two people to carry them safely. Since most attic walkways are regulated for 250 pounds, there's absolutely no chance you'll be able to carry a new unit up to your attic (assuming that's where it is) and install it successfully without destroying your unit and hurting yourself in the process. Moreover, if your home runs on gas, it may actually be illegal for you to work on your home's HVAC system. Nearly every state in the country requires technicians to carry a permit to work on gas lines, precisely because of their flammable nature. The last thing you want is somebody who doesn't know what they're doing messing around with the gas lines inside your home. Assuming they don't explode outright, they can leak poisonous carbon monoxide throughout your home that could be fatal.

Does this mean you should never work on your HVAC system? Absolutely not! Fortunately for all of us, contractors make the areas that require regular maintenance easily accessible. All you need is a stepladder and a few materials and you're off to the races.

Below is a list of some of the most common HVAC items you need to pay attention to as a homeowner. This assumes that your unit is functioning correctly; if it isn't, call a technician to have it looked at immediately.

- **Replace air filters.** On average, you should replace the air filters inside your home every 60 to 90 days (more often if you have pets or family members with allergy problems). Most homes have one air filter, but you may have two if you have a larger home or a second story. Replacing them is a snap; simply find the metal grate that is in your home, undo the latches, pull the old filter out, and replace it with the new one. The hardest part of this process will be determining the right size for your filter, which annoyingly can result in several trips to the hardware store until you get it right. If you notice gunk collecting on the outside of the vents, take a duster and knock all that off as well.

- **Get it inspected.** Ideally, you should have your whole HVAC system inspected professionally every year. For most homeowners, that's a laughable concept, especially considering how much they pay to keep the other systems in the house running efficiently. However, spending $200 on an inspection may be one of the best investments you ever make in your house, as an inspection can determine whether or not repairs need to be made or if the unit is about to fail completely. Often times, a simple repair can have your unit running for another year or two, saving you a lot of money on a new unit. Alternatively, if you delay having your system inspected, it could fail completely on a really hot or cold day, leaving your family in a potentially dangerous situation. Scheduling an inspection can be easy to overlook but put it on your schedule during the transition periods (late spring or early fall) every year.

- **Reduce your usage.** It's a simple fact: the harder your system works, the shorter life it will have. The average AC unit is rated to operate at a steady 75 degrees, so if you're one of those people that likes to keep your home around 65 during the hottest days of summer, you can expect to spring for a new air conditioning system much sooner than others. That may be worth it to you, but there's also a way to keep your home at the right temperature while reducing the strain on your system. Using dark, heavy curtains will trap in the cool, while adding higher-efficiency fans can improve the airflow and take the strain off your unit. Adding extra insulation to your house and adjusting the thermostat to rest when you're not at home for long periods can help as well. Smart thermostats can track when you're not in the house and will turn the temperature either up or down, depending on the season, to reduce strain on your system. Just make sure you set it to adjust an hour or two before you come home, or else it can be uncomfortable when you walk in the door.

- **Keep it clean.** One of the fastest ways to blow out your HVAC system is by allowing clogs to develop. You can keep this from happening with a simple visual inspection. Walk outside and inspect your heating and air conditioning units; if there's debris in the way, simply dislodge it. If you find you have to do this often, you may want to erect a permanent barrier of sorts to protect your units. The same goes for any air vents in your house. If any of them are blocked, clear the blockage immediately.

- **Listen for weird noises.** Most likely, you'll be able to tell pretty quickly if your HVAC system is not functioning properly. A squealing, clanking, or rattling sound emanating through your vents can indicate a bolt has fallen off or that the belt in your motor is about to snap. Any weird noises from your HVAC system warrant a call to your local HVAC technician as soon as possible.

Before we close this chapter, I want to mention one more thing I alluded to earlier: home maintenance plans. Generally speaking, you can contact your local HVAC company to set up a maintenance plan that will allow them to do all of this (and sometimes more) for a standard yearly cost. These plans can be expensive — usually ranging from $500 to $2000 a year — but if you're the type of person that would prefer to take a hands-off approach to your home, it could be worth it. They'll handle any type of maintenance that needs to be done, such as changing air filters and clearing the debris, while also performing routine inspections and checkups. The cost may even include a tune-up, which can help your HVAC system run for several years longer, and if any repairs or replacements need to be performed, they'll most likely offer those to you at a discount. If you're interested, contact your local HVAC company for more information.

CHAPTER 12:

HOW TO PREP
FOR A DISASTER

We would be remiss if we closed out this book and didn't mention one of the biggest things that can happen to your house at any time: natural disasters. While there is virtually no way to make your home 100% bulletproof from anything that could ever happen, there are many different steps that you can and should take to prevent a disaster from becoming absolute.

Probably the hardest thing about natural disasters is that they can spring up with virtually no warning whatsoever. Of course, that can change depending on what type of disaster it is and what part of the world you live in. Certain parts of the United States, such as the West Coast, are more prone to earthquakes, while those in the South generally deal with hurricanes and tornadoes. The difference between these types of disasters can be huge; hurricanes are usually forecasted a week or so in advance, while an earthquake can spring up within seconds.

No matter which disaster you're dealing with, the best course of action is to prepare yourself against just about anything you know you may experience. In this chapter, we've listed out three of the most common natural disasters, but the same principles that apply to these three can apply to just about anything else you may experience. The stakes are real here, too; failure to plan now can quite literally be the difference between life and death.

If you don't have one already, you should look into creating your own "disaster kit." Once again, the contents may change depending on the disaster, but most disaster kits have the following: a whistle for every member of your family, blankets, batteries, a three-day water supply, two days' worth of food, a first aid kit, a flashlight, and a weather radio. For extra disaster preparedness, keep one of these in each of your cars, too.

You should also consider investing in a generator. These act like portable power stations that can keep your phones, refrigerator, and even your television operational when the power goes completely out. Most models rely on gas to operate, so you also want to get a gas can and fill it to store in your garage. If you do, though, *be VERY careful not to ever run the generator inside*. In just about every disaster scenario in the country where fatalities are concerned, there are usually a couple that result from a generator being powered inside. Carbon monoxide from the engine slowly leaks out into the room, poisoning everybody in that space. If you're going to use a gas-powered generator, *ALWAYS* put it outside, and run the power lines through a door or window. If you don't mind spending a little bit more money, you can always look into a battery-powered generator which is substantially safer.

Once you have the necessary ingredients for your disaster kit, gather your family and craft a disaster plan. You should all know where the main shut-off valves are for water, gas, and electricity. Also, every single person should familiarize themselves with the evacuation plan in case of an emergency. Some families like to run drills a couple of times a year to familiarize themselves with what to do, which isn't a bad idea either. Make sure you also have one for your pets. While the rest of your family may keep a level head, your pets will have no idea what's going on and can be extremely bothered. In my experience, it's always best to let one of the older kids be responsible for the family dog. It gives them an important job, while also providing necessary distraction during an extremely turbulent time.

One more thing: while you don't necessarily need to have these in your disaster kit, you should also print off a copy of your insurance documents and keep them in a secure place. Alternatively, you can upload them to a device or cloud-based storage, but they need to be easily accessible no matter where they are. Once the disaster is over, these will be paramount to helping you rebuild.

Now, let's talk about some basic steps to prepare for the most likely natural disasters you may face. Remember, these are just guidelines. For more information, visit your local government's website, or ask your neighbors and community leaders what steps you can take in addition. The more you prepare, the "easier" your experience will be.

Hurricanes

For those that live in coastal areas, such as Florida or the Carolinas, hurricanes are probably a normal fact of life. If you've grown up in those areas, you most likely remember watching your parents board up the windows and bring all the outdoor furniture inside when the hurricane was approaching, so preparing your home for a hurricane may be second nature. If you've moved from elsewhere, though, you'll need to prepare yourself for a rough few days.

Fortunately, hurricanes can be predicted several days in advance because they can last several days more, and most people will need that time to prepare adequately. This means that you need to have a long-term strategy to cope with the situation. Gas up your vehicle, clear the debris outside, secure the windows and doors by putting wood up to block debris, and have enough food and water to last for several days.

One other threat to be aware of during a hurricane is flash flooding. The amount of water dumped on an individual area can be astronomical, sometimes creating floodwaters that reach 10 to 15 feet or more in height. If you can, elevate your furniture to prevent it from getting water damage, and put sandbags around your cars to prevent water from destroying them. Move most of your important possessions to high ground and have an evacuation plan if the home itself is flooded. Keep a weather radio and communicate with your local officials, paying close attention to any evacuation orders they issue. You'll also want an alternative route in case the main thoroughfares are clogged (which they almost always are).

Tornadoes

If you've never seen a tornado in person, it can be a frightening experience. Few things are more terrifying than watching a several-thousand-foot-tall wall of wind move slowly toward you, picking up and throwing everything in its path. Although most tornadoes are not the massive F5 twisters you see depicted in movies, just about every tornado has the power to damage your home and injure your family, so you must take them all seriously.

Barring anything else, the one thing you need if you live in tornado country is a designated safe room. These are generally reinforced closets that can withstand the impact of debris as it slams up against the wall and can even be subterranean. They can get expensive—$3000 to $5000 each—but if a tornado is bearing down on you, you'll be thanking your lucky stars you have one. If you don't have a safe room, find an interior closet or room you can run to, and make sure everybody in the household knows where it is.

Keep your eye on the news if you see a tornado watch appearing in your area and have a plan if a tornado develops. If you're outdoors when one happens, find the lowest spot possible and avoid trees and cars that can act as missiles. You'll also want a disaster survival kit containing many of the same items listed above in your safe room, ready to use if necessary. Also, it's smart to have a means of communicating with the outside world. Debris can be piled up outside of your door, trapping you inside. Having a way to interact with first responders that will sift through the rubble can save your life.

Earthquakes

If you happen to live in an area prone to earthquakes, there's virtually no warning about when these might show up, so it's best to prepare beforehand. The best way to do that is to tie down anything that can fall: refrigerators, bookcases, TVs, and picture frames, among others. You don't necessarily have to have long, ugly ropes holding everything in place, either; most hardware stores offer straps that can be discreetly tied to the wall behind the unit. Take advantage of them.

Because earthquakes can happen so fast, everyone in your household, including yourself, needs to know instinctively what to do if an earthquake hits. Remember the three steps: drop, cover, and hold on. Find a doorway or a table to duck under, hold onto something—especially if you live in a second or third-floor apartment—and ride it out. Earthquakes don't usually last long, but they can be terrifying. There's nothing you can do except sit tight.

If you find yourself trapped, use your phone to send a text message to friends and loved ones with your exact GPS location. If you don't have your phone, bang on a pipe or anything else you can find to make as much noise as possible. Save your strength, since it may take time for first responders to get to you but try to make noise every 5 to 10 minutes so you can alert people nearby. If you hear voices, make as much noise as possible.

Regardless of what type of natural disaster you experience, it's important to avoid the dangers that can happen after the disaster is over. Downed power lines can be lethal, as are water "puddles" in the road. Since you don't know if the ground underneath has shifted, it could be a lot deeper than you think. You should also be ready for secondary effects, such as aftershocks and falling debris. Stick together with your family, have a plan, and know what you'll do during a disaster, and you'll give yourself the best chance at survival.

CHAPTER 13:

HOW TO SAVE ON REGULAR EXPENSES

The subject of budgeting could take up not just one book but an entire library. There is not nearly enough space here to do the issue any type of justice, so I will try to hit the high points here and keep it all as basic as possible. Keep in mind, I am a "first-time homebuyer survival guide expert," not an accountant, so be sure to follow up with professionals if you have additional questions.

Just like we have in the rest of this book, I'm going to assume you already have a house picked out and paid for, which means that you don't need any help negotiating mortgage prices or closing costs and that you already understand the value of shopping around to find the best offer. You probably already have those expenses baked into your existing monthly payment, so instead, we're going to talk about the best ways to lower those payments that are already on the house.

The reasons for lowering them can vary from person to person. For first-time homebuyers who have taken advantage of some of the incentives, you may want to remove some of the taxes that can go along with home ownership, such as private mortgage insurance, which can be a couple of hundred dollars a month. Alternatively, you may decide to speed up your process by moving from a 30-year fixed mortgage to a 15-year fixed mortgage, even though you'll pay more every month. Most commonly, people just want to have lower payments to have more discretionary income to spend in everyday life. There's nothing wrong with that, of course, just make sure that you're not setting yourself up for a harder road in the future.

At its most simple, three major items add up to your "monthly" payment: property taxes, home insurance, and your mortgage. Your mortgage is your loan balance, property taxes are what you owe your local municipality for having a home in their area, and the insurance is the payment required by law and your lender to cover you if something happens to your home. All three of these can be negotiated separately or together, depending on which approach you take. If you're the type of person that likes to nitpick between the three different areas to get the lowest rate, then, by all means, negotiate them individually. If you'd rather have a more streamlined process and simply pay them all in one lump payment, then your lender can most likely help with that as well. The choice is yours.

If you decide to handle them all individually, you'll need more budgeting skills to make sure that you stay up to date on your premiums. While property taxes can fluctuate from year to year, you should have a pretty good estimation of what they'll be when your city sends you a letter during the annual appraisal process. You always have the option to appeal this letter but expect a substantial amount of resistance and varying degrees of success. As a rule of thumb, you should always plan to pay whatever you paid last year, plus 10%. Homeowner taxes generally don't rise more than that year after year.

So, let's get granular here for a moment, starting with your mortgage, which will undoubtedly be your biggest monthly expense.

Mortgage

Generally speaking, your mortgage will consume more than half of your monthly income, and sometimes up to 75%. So, any amount you can reduce this will inevitably have a bigger and more positive net effect on your total. The easiest way to lower your payment is to simply extend the terms. Moving your mortgage from a 15-year note to a 30-year note will save you several hundred dollars a month, depending on your mortgage cost. You should expect to pay a small fee to have the mortgage company process it for you, but the bigger concern is the amount you will pay in interest. If you extend your mortgage from 15 to 30 years, you could be paying three or even four times the amount of money overall in interest payments alone, so make sure you're okay with that before you decide to refinance. If 30 years isn't enough, some companies even offer 45- or 60-year mortgage terms. As expected, with these, you lower your monthly payment, but you will owe an astronomical amount of money in interest.

You can also refinance your home. Doing so is a slightly more complicated process, and you should take into account the economic climate before you do it to ensure you'll have a better interest rate. But, if you can save 1 to 2 percentage points on your interest, that can add up to thousands of dollars over the life of your loan. You'll have to get a new appraisal done, which can be around $500. Refinancing will reset the clock on your mortgage (taking you back to 30 years, for example, if you have a 30-year note), but it could be worth it. Shop around to different lenders and get the best rate possible to see if it makes financial sense.

Another alternative to home refinancing is to do what's called a "cash-out refinancing." "Cash-out Refinancing" allows you to restructure or consolidate your loan to include other debts you may have, such as credit cards, car loans, or even tuition. This approach leaves you with one simple payment every month and can even allow you to take out extra cash for other projects. A home equity line of credit (HELOC) can achieve the same type of thing, but in that situation, you're taking out a loan against your house, which means that if you default, the lender could put a lien against your home. You'll also have another payment to make every month.

As mentioned earlier, one of the other things you should look into, especially if you have taken advantage of a first-time homeowner loan, is the elimination of private mortgage insurance. This additional cost is put in place by lenders if you don't put down 20% as a down payment, which is the case with many people. PMI is an extra payment every month to ensure the lender in case you default on your loan, but once you hit 20% equity, you have the option of dropping the PMI from your payment, and you should absolutely take advantage of it. Don't count on your lender to drop it for you since that's money out of their pocket. You'll have to take the initiative and call them yourselves.

Property Taxes

Since every municipality measures these differently, it's hard to issue blanket statements concerning property taxes. For example, if you live in a growing town, you can expect your property taxes to increase every year as the city allocates more funds to help with roads, water lines, and other infrastructure needed for developmental purposes. By contrast, if the town is getting smaller or less economic activity, you should fight to have your property taxes lowered by voting for certain proposals or appealing your current rate directly. Appeals may or may not be successful, but they're at least worth a shot.

If those measures don't work, there are still options. You can always scale back property improvements to your home, such as deciding against that extra bedroom or in-ground pool. Doing so will cause your property value to remain where it is, but you'll also miss out on the material benefits of the improvements, so you'll have to weigh your priorities on an individual basis. You can also look for tax exemptions from the government if you have energy-efficient fixtures, such as solar panels or green building materials. If all else fails, it never hurts to get a second opinion to reevaluate your home. Walking through it with a tax appraiser and pointing out all the negative aspects of your house may result in a lower value, which will also decrease your taxes.

Homeowner's Insurance

Homeowner's insurance operates exactly like any other form of insurance (health, dental, auto, etc.). It can be negotiated, bundled, paid in advance, or anything else your insurer allows, and all you need to do is talk to them. They may have different programs or plans now that you didn't know about when you first bought your home that can significantly reduce your overall insurance bill.

Probably the quickest way to make an impact on your monthly payments is to raise your deductible. You might have to pay more in the event of a disaster, since you'll have less coverage, so it's definitely a risk. It's much easier to simply bundle your home and auto insurance together and get a lower rate. Or do both; it's up to you.

Since insurance is created to protect against unforeseen events, creating a more "defensible" home may also allow you to take advantage of lower rates. Security systems can sometimes make a difference, as can certain structural improvements to make your home more resistant to natural disasters. It's up to the individual insurer to make these types of calls, so make sure you talk to yours before investing in these activities.

CHAPTER 14:

HOW TO KNOW WHAT ADDS VALUE AND WHAT DOESN'T

There are two types of homeowners: those who look at their home as a stepping stone to financial improvement and those who pour their heart and soul into it their investment with hopes of making it their dream home. Despite how these two stances sound, neither is inherently better than the other. Many people begin the home buying process as a means to a different end. Fortunately or unfortunately, they soon find that the home they bought, thinking they would only live in temporarily, is the home they retire in 50 years later. It just depends on your priorities in life and where your path takes you.

Ultimately, it doesn't matter what your goal is for purchasing a home; it's a financial investment, and it needs to be treated as such. Because of that, you should be crystal clear about what you want to get out of the improvements you make to your home. If you're adding a bathroom because your daughter needs her own private space, that's one thing, but if you're adding it hoping it will improve the resale value down the road, that's a different matter entirely. Remember, almost nothing you do to your house will completely recoup your *actual* investment. What I mean by that is that if you put $10,000 into an improvement in your home, you rarely get that *same* $10,000 back when you try to sell it. There are exceptions, of course, but that's the general rule.

That's not to say you can't recoup *most* of your investment. In addition to the ability to enjoy the improvements while you live there, some investments can net you 80 to 90% down the road. Those are the investments we should be making all the time because they both serve our immediate purpose and our long-term need as well.

Conversely, there are other adjustments we can make to our homes that decrease the original value.

Converting a bedroom into an office is a great idea, especially in a post-Covid world, where working from home is more commonplace. However, losing that extra bedroom may cost you if a potential home buyer decides it's not big enough for their family. Not everyone works from home (or wants to), so you have to think long and hard before converting a space to something else.

In the end, though, it doesn't entirely matter why you make the investments you do for your home. If you do them simply because you want to, then, by all means, turn your home into whatever your heart desires. Add in the fixtures, tear out walls, and put a Ferris wheel in your backyard if you want to. The beauty of owning your own home is that you can do whatever you want with your space, and nobody can tell you otherwise.

What actually adds value to your home can vary from design to design, but there are a few principles that govern whether or not certain things will add more value to your home than others.

- **It makes your home prettier**. Curb appeal is absolutely essential to home value, so siding, deck additions, larger front porches, or landscaping can really add up. A front yard that just looks absolutely gorgeous will almost always net more money than the same house with a terrible looking yard.

- **It adds more space to your home.** Converting your garage into an extra bedroom can add a huge boost to resale value and is relatively easy to do with just about any contractor. Of course, you'll have to find a place to park your cars. Potential homebuyers may not appreciate that aspect of it, but there's no doubt adding an extra 800 ft.² to your house can add to your bottom line.

- **It increases your home's energy efficiency.** Lighting, appliances, and solar panels all add to a higher resale value, especially because potential homebuyers know they won't have to spend as much on utilities and will probably gain tax exemptions in the process. While you probably shouldn't add energy-efficient appliances months before you move to simply boost the resale value, if you know you're going to have to replace them anyway, do so with higher efficiency units.

- **It makes your home smarter.** The ability to monitor your home, lock your doors, and turn on your lights from a smart phone is becoming more invaluable, and potential homebuyers will eat it up with a spoon. Since many people don't have the time or the energy to learn what goes into making a home "smart," if it's already done for them, they'll be more than happy to hand over a few extra dollars for your trouble.

If you decide to go the route of making large-scale structural improvements to your home, you'll most likely have to work with at least one contractor. Most of these people are trustworthy, and in my experience, a good contractor will save you a ton of money over the project and will communicate with you every step of the way. It's only fair, though, that you learn how to work with them as well. If they're going to communicate with you, you need to know how to communicate what you want to them. Doing so will make everyone's jobs easier.

Before you decide to hire a specific contractor, make sure you ask for recommendations from people you trust and get multiple quotes about the same project. You may have to walk the same space or make the same phone call a dozen times, but if you can shave a few hundred dollars off your end price, it may be worth it in the end. Also, watch out for "allowances." These line items are nothing more than placeholders in your budget that allow flex space for a contractor to insert something later. If, however, you leave $300 as an "allowance" for a lighting fixture, and the contractor only ends up spending $100, then that $200 will most likely end up in their pocket. It doesn't always seem fair, but it's also not completely unethical either. Contractors have a lot of overhead themselves, and most of the time, numbers like this get lost in the shuffle. Make sure every item is specified within your unique budget and track the expenses, so you don't end up spending more than you need to.

Make sure you also vet contractors using online reviews. Look on Home Advisor, Angie's List, or even Google to see what other people's experiences have been with them in the past, especially as it pertains to your specific project. Even better, let them know you'll be leaving them a review. In some cases, you may get them to throw in a few extra pieces in exchange for them using pictures of your project on their website portfolio.

Before the project even starts, try to get a schedule in writing. You should know, from day-to-day, what type of work will be taking place inside your house. This isn't only so you can keep tabs on them but also so you can remove items and get out of their way while the work is taking place. Honestly, you won't *want* to be in their way, so giving you a schedule of their activities is in their best interest as well. Check the work often throughout the project and communicate any issues you may have as soon as you spot them. The deeper they go on a project, the harder it will be to undo the work and make it right.

Finally, never pay until the project is complete. Once you hand over the money, that's an assumption the contract has been fulfilled, and the contractor is not obligated to do anything else (unless specified in the contract). Don't be afraid to make them fix whatever it is that was done incorrectly. That doesn't mean you necessarily need to play "hardball" with them but stand your ground and be insistent about it. It's your house, and you're paying for certain improvements. They need to fulfill their end of the bargain.

Having a solid contractor in your back pocket is invaluable. Having someone on standby, you can talk to and get quotes from regularly will help you make better decisions about your home as to what's feasible and what's not.

CHAPTER 15:

HOW TO MAINTAIN YOUR HOME

I threw a lot at you in this book so far, and hopefully, it will help you be the most prepared homeowner on your block. Most people buy the keys to their home, walk in, set up shop, and continue life as normal, but by keeping a steady eye on your home, you'll be able to not only recoup that investment down the road but also enjoy it for years to come.

I know how much I wish I had a book like this when I started my home-owning journey. Something easily accessible, short, and packed with information I needed to know from the day that I walked in with the keys to the day I walked out would've been enormously helpful. I hope you see this book in the same way.

In order to keep as efficient as possible, I wanted to create a simple checklist of all the things you need to do regularly to keep your home spick-and-span. I've tried to divvy it up in a way that makes the most sense, but in no way should you ever look at this schedule as ironclad. It's nothing more than a guideline for you to build off, so don't be afraid to add things to the schedule over time.

I also made sure not to include everything in this book since not everything needs to be dictated on a schedule. Some things you'll spot and take care of at the moment, and others you'll call a technician to fix when you notice there's an issue. By and large, though, this list encompasses most of the things every homeowner needs to have on their yearly schedule.

Every Month

- **Check your furnace filter,** especially in the cold months. Having a furnace that can filter air through your home is not only a good idea for energy efficiency but could also protect you from a fire. It takes only a few minutes to check and a few more to replace if necessary.

- **Clean faucet heads.** Scaly buildup is inevitable on all your faucets, bathtubs, sinks, and showers, so take a little bit of time to unscrew all the caps and clean them off. Few things are more disgusting than ignoring this for several years, only to have them clog up on you completely. Then, when you unscrew them, you see a whole ecosystem living inside.

- **Test smoke alarms.** Depending on how many you have, this should only take a few minutes, but be sure to go around to every single one (including your carbon monoxide detectors) and press the test button to wait for the sound. If you don't hear anything, change the batteries.

- **Clean garbage disposal.** There are all sorts of online DIY tutorials for this, but it's a really simple process. Take a few basic ingredients, mix them, turn on the hot water, and allow them to run down the drain together. It'll clean the disposal as well as your pipes.

Every Three Months

- **Test your garage door.** Most people never think about the garage doors until they stop working, but as a part of your quarterly maintenance schedule, test the safety mechanisms on your door and listen for any sounds that indicate your door is about to fail. Lubricate the tracks and tighten any bolts if necessary.

- **Replace AC filter.** If you have pets or family members with breathing issues, you may want to move this to every two months, but at the very least, your air conditioning filter needs to be traded out every 90 days. You can get a higher quality filter that will remove more of the allergens, but that doesn't mean it can stay in longer. Every three months, replace the AC filter.

- **Run unused faucets.** Any faucets or tubs that aren't regularly used should be turned on for about 15 seconds every three months to keep water flowing through them. If there's no water running to the pipes, clogs can build up quicker, causing major problems. Running them regularly will help alleviate the issue.

Every Six Months

- **Deep clean your house**. Hopefully, you're keeping your house relatively clean all the time, but every six months, it's a good idea to go throughout your home and deep clean the baseboards, carpet, fan blades, and anything else you see. This will keep dust from getting into vents and electrical sockets and promote overall health and happiness.

- **Clean refrigerator coils.** This isn't a really big job, but it can be a headache if you've never done it before. Simply pull your refrigerator out from the wall so you can slide behind it and wipe down the coils you see on the back. This will prevent gunk buildup from causing the coils to freeze, which results in a bricked refrigerator.

Every Fall

- **Aerate the lawn.** Before your yard starts to go to sleep for a long winter's nap, you'll need to aerate the lawn to allow it to breathe a little bit. You can use a manual aeration machine, rent one from your local hardware store, or buy a liquid aeration solution. Doing so will help revitalize your lawn when it comes back in the spring.

- **Schedule HVAC inspection.** Technically speaking, you can do this in either the spring or the fall, but it's always a good idea to have it done during the transition times of the year before a new system kicks on. Check vents, air ducts, and the units themselves to ensure they are in proper working order and fix any problems you may see.

- **Touch up siding.** Walk around the outside of your house and examine the state of your siding. If there are cracks or holes, patch those up and re-paint those parts. If there's dirt build-up, grab the power washer and spray it all down to have it looking sharp for the wintertime.

- **Clean the gutters.** If you're scared of heights, feel free to hire this out, but every year, you'll need to manually clean out the gutters to keep leaves and gunk from clogging them up. If you don't clean the gutters, water will pool on the edge of the roof and eat away at the shingles, causing a leak.

- **Winterize exterior plumbing.** Before the temperature starts to drop, put a cover over the faucet and wrap any exterior pipes in heat tape to keep them from freezing. You can do the same with interior pipes that are located in the attic and basement. Make sure you cover ones that are directly exposed to the cold.

- **Vacuum dryer lint.** The filter on your dryer does a great job of picking up most of the lit, but debris will inevitably come through the exhaust pipe in the back and eventually spit out from the top of your house. If it doesn't, it'll get clogged, and if it gets clogged, it can start a fire. Clean it out once a year to keep that from happening.

- **Put pre-emergent on the lawn.** You want to do this when the soil temp drops below 55, as that's the time that pre-emergent takes root. This will prevent any weed seeds from germinating over the winter and then springing up as your grass comes back to life several months from now.

- **Seal the grout.** Inspect your windows and door frames for any gaps, and re-seal them with caulk if necessary. This will increase your energy efficiency and make it more comfortable to live during the cold winter.

Every Spring

- **Clean the carpets.** Since you've been inside for the last several months due to the cold weather, it's a good idea to have the carpets deep cleaned to pick up any residue that may have been trampled inside. Not only will they look better, but deep cleaning will also preserve the mat underneath as well.

- **Start outdoor projects.** As soon as the weather is agreeable, start gathering the tools and resources necessary to start any outdoor projects, such as getting the lawn back into shape, replacing fence and deck posts, or starting a garden. This is the perfect time to do all those.

- **Lay down pre-emergent.** Once the soil temperature starts to hit 55, put down another layer of pre-emergent. This is also a great time to get your fertilizer schedule going. About every 4 to 6 weeks, lay down an organic fertilizer in addition to your weekly mowing.

- **Inspect for cracks.** Do a visual inspection of your house and look at the bricks in the foundation. Call a foundation repairman if you spot any cracks and get them fixed, otherwise, you could be paying for a full replacement down the road.

This list is exhaustive by no means, but it'll hopefully provide you with a good starting point as you begin your journey on being a homeowner. Remember, if you take care of your house, it'll take care of you!

ONE FINAL WORD

As a final farewell, let me leave you with one closing thought: *take pride in your home*. Too many people buy a house because they feel like it's what they're supposed to do, or they think that it makes the most financial "sense." In reality, buying a house is a point of pride for not only you and your family but also the entire neighborhood. As a part of a community, you take an unspoken oath to maintain and upkeep your house for the betterment of the entire area. That's a responsibility that we should all take very seriously.

It's also something you can take a lot of pleasure in. Having your own little slice of land that you're free to create and build on, as well as tend, goes in line with what I believe are some of our most basic responsibilities as human beings. It's not always just about keeping your utilities low and selling your home for the most resale value. It's about contributing to the overall good. Call me sappy, but that's just one of the reasons why I enjoy owning a home.

Of course, home ownership can always be a point of pride. Whether you have a family or not, the fact remains that at some point, people will walk through your front door and form an opinion about you that is unmistakably connected to your home. Your sense of style and your basic managerial habits are on full display for everyone to see, so you might as well make the most of it.

Overall, we can go through all the checklists and fundamentals of being a first-time homeowner, but if you don't love your house, then it's all for nothing. You will instinctively know what needs to be done and what needs to be taken care of, but this is a guide to some of the more unseen things, the ones people learn along the way. Feel free to add to this list, especially as you guide other future homeowners in their journey, and share this with them if you feel like it's helped you.

All the best, first-time homeowner, and good luck!

Made in United States
Troutdale, OR
04/10/2024

19090829R00070